*the*
# JOHN LENNON
*family album*

*the*
# JOHN LENNON
*family album*

Nishi F. Saimaru

Chronicle Books • San Francisco

First published in the United States 1990 by
Chronicle Books.

*The John Lennon Family Album* was originally published
in 1982 by Kadokawa Shoten (Tokyo) and in 1990 by
Shogakukan (Tokyo).

Editors: Makoto Nagano, Kohei Kitayama, Ken
Sekiguchi, Tetsuo Saijo (Fly Communications) and
Shuji Shimamoto (Shogakukan).
Art Director: Katsumi Asaba


Printed in Japan.

**Library of Congress Cataloging in Publication Data**

Saimaru, Nishi Fumiya.
    [Jon Renon kazoku seikatsu. English]
    The John Lennon family album / photography by Nishi F.
Saimaru.
        p.      cm.
    Translation of: Jon Renon kazoku seikatsu.
    ISBN 0-87701-804-9
    1. Lennon, John, 1940–1980 / Portraits.    2. Ono, Yōko — Portraits.
I. Title.
    ML88.L36S2   1990
    779'.978242166' 0922 — dc20          90-46007
                                           CIP
                                         MN

Cover design: Brenda Rae Eno
Cover photograph: Nishi F. Saimaru

Distributed in Canada by Raincoast Books,
112 East Third Avenue, Vancouver, B.C. V5T 1C8

10  9  8  7  6  5  4  3  2  1

Chronicle Books
275 Fifth Street
San Francisco, CA 94103

## Table of Contents

# A Love Letter from John and Yoko to People Who Ask Us What, When, and Why

The past 10 years we noticed everything we wished came true in its own time, good or bad, one way or the other. We kept telling each other that one of these days we would have to get organized and wish for only good things. Then our baby arrived! We were overjoyed and at the same time felt very responsible. Now our wishes would also affect *him*. We felt it was time for us to stop discussing and do something about our wishing process: The Spring Cleaning of our minds! It was a lot of work. We kept finding things in those old closets in our minds that we hadn't realized were still there, things we wished we hadn't found. As we did our cleaning, we also started to notice many wrong things in our house: there was a shelf which should never have been there in the first place, a painting we grew to dislike, and there were the two dingy rooms, which became light and breezy when we broke the walls between them. We started to love the plants, which one of us originally thought were robbing the air from us! We began to enjoy the drum beat of the city which used to annoy us. We made a lot of mistakes and still do. In the past we spent a lot of energy in trying to get something we thought we wanted, wondered why we didn't get it, only to find out that one or both of us didn't really want it. One day, we received a sudden rain of chocolates from people around the world. "Hey, what's this! We're not eating sugar stuff, are we?" "Who's wishing it?" We both laughed. We discovered that when two of us wished in unison, it happened faster. As the Good Book says— Where two are gathered together—It's true. Two is plenty. A Newclear Seed.

More and more we are starting to wish and pray. The things we have tried to achieve in the past by flashing a V sign, we try now through wishing. We are not doing this because it is simpler. Wishing is more effective than waving flags. It works. It's like magic. Magic is simple. Magic is real. The secret of it is to know that it is simple, and not kill it with an elaborate ritual which is a sign of insecurity. When somebody is angry with us, we draw a halo around his or her head in our minds. Does the person stop being angry then? Well, we don't know! We know, though, that when we draw a halo around a person, suddenly the person starts to look like an angel to us. This helps us to feel warm towards the person, reminds us that everyone has goodness inside, and that all people who come to us are angels in disguise, carrying messages and gifts to us from the Universe. Magic is logical. Try it sometime. We still have a long way to go. It seems the more we get into cleaning, the faster the wishing and receiving process gets. The house is getting very comfortable now. Sean is beautiful. The plants are growing. The cats are purring. The town is shining, sun, rain or snow. We live in a beautiful universe. We are thankful every day for the plentifulness of our life. This is not a euphemism. We understand that we, the city, the country, the earth are facing very hard times, and there is panic in the air. Still the sun is shining and we are here together, and there is love between us, our city, the country, the earth. If two people like us can do what we are doing with our lives, any miracle is possible! It's true we can do with a few big miracles right now. The thing is to recognize them when they come to you and to be thankful. First they come in a small way, in every day, life, then they come in rivers, and in oceans. It's goin' to be alright! The future of the earth is up to all of us.

Many people are sending us vibes every day in letters, telegrams, taps on the gate, or just flowers and nice thoughts. We thank them all and appreciate them for respecting our quiet space, which we need. Thank you for all the love you send us. We feel it every day. We love you, too. We know you are concerned about us. That is nice. That's why you want to know what we are doing. That's why everybody is asking us What, When and Why. We understand. Well, this is what we've been doing. We hope that you have the same quiet space in your mind to make your own wishes come true.


If you think of us next time, remember, our silence is a silence of love and not of indifference. Remember, we are writing in the sky instead of on paper — that's our song. Lift your eyes and look up in the sky. There's our message. Lift your eyes again and look around you, and you will see that you are walking in the sky, which extends to the ground. We are all part of the sky, more so than of the ground. Remember, we love you.


John Lennon & Yoko Ono
May 27th, 1979
*New York City*


P.S. We noticed that three angels were looking over our shoulders when we wrote this!

*Spring 1977*

John, Yoko, and Sean at the New
Marlboro, Massachusetts, farm of
artist George Maciunas. Sean is
seventeen months old.

*New Marlboro, Massachusetts,*
*March 1977.*

Sean's governess looks on while John and Sean slide
down the hill in front of George's house. George
Maciunas is in the background.

*New Marlboro, Massachusetts,*
*March 1977.*


Another family photo, with two of
George's dogs.

*New Marlboro, Massachusetts,*
*March 1977.*

Sean, John, and Yoko pose on a sunny, cold day.

*New Marlboro, Massachusetts, March 1977.*

In Monterey, a town not far from New Marlboro, John, Yoko, and George Maciunas dressed up in Old West costumes in a photo studio.

*Monterey, Massachusetts, March 1977.*

In Madison Square Garden, John and
Sean are entranced by a flying trapeze
act during a Ringling Brothers circus.

*New York City,*
*April 1977.*

While watching the circus, John was spotted by ABC television; the interview was broadcast on the evening news.

*New York City,*
*April 1977.*

At the circus, Mick Jagger unexpectedly
dropped by to say hello to John, Yoko,
and Sean.

*New York City,*
*April 1977.*

# Summer 1977

Holding Sean atop a hill during a family trip to Hong Kong, John looks pleased to be an anonymous tourist.

*Hong Kong,*
*June 1977.*

Wearing the hat he bought for Sean to ward off the heat, John clowns in front of one of the sculptures in Tiger Balm Garden.

*Hong Kong,*
*June 1977.*

John poses with Sean in Tiger Balm Garden.

*Hong Kong,*
*June 1977.*

John leads Sean through Tiger Balm Garden.

*Hong Kong,*
*June 1977.*

John strolls around Hong Kong with Sean. Not many
people recognized him, but occasionally a tourist
from the West would say, "Aren't you John Lennon?"
John would reply, "I get told that a lot."

*Hong Kong,*
*June 1977.*

John and Sean on a double-decker bus, looking tired after a long day of sightseeing.

*Hong Kong,*
*June 1977.*

While being held by his governess at a
Hong Kong restaurant, Sean fails to
notice his father's antics.

*Hong Kong,*
*June 1977.*

Sean runs around the hotel room while John is lost
in thought. Later that day, we ran into David Bowie
in the Mandarin Hotel lobby on his way back from
Japan and joined him for dinner.

*Hong Kong,*
*June 1977.*

John and Sean gaze at the sunset on a
ferry to Nine Dragon Island.

*Hong Kong,*
*June 1977.*

John, Yoko, and Sean with the Ono family in the garden of a Tokyo guesthouse.

*Tokyo, Japan, summer 1977.*

Wheeling Sean through Tokyo's Ueno Zoo, John is
spotted by students on a field trip.

*Tokyo, Japan,
July 1977.*

John holds Sean up to get a better look
at the elephants at Tokyo's Ueno Zoo.

*Tokyo, Japan,*
*July 1977.*

During the summer of 1977, the Lennon family stayed in an old hotel in the historic resort town of Karuizawa, 75 miles northwest of Tokyo. Here, John and Yoko take a break during their morning routine of cycling.

*Karuizawa, Japan,*
*summer 1977.*

Sean rides along with John on one
of their many bicycle outings in
Karuizawa.

*Karuizawa, Japan,*
*summer 1977.*

A family portrait.    *Karuizawa, Japan, summer 1977.*

On a short trip from Karuizawa, the Lennon family visits Onioshidashi,
a popular spot on Asama Mountain.   *Japan, summer 1977.*

John poses with Sean in Onioshidashi.    *Japan, summer 1977.*

John snaps pictures of Sean with a Polaroid camera while Yoko and her mother look on.

*Japan,*
*summer 1977.*

On the drive to Onioshidashi, John tries to show Sean how to look through a telescope but Sean is distracted.     *Japan, summer 1977.*

On the drive to Onioshidashi.  *Japan, summer 1977.*

At a restaurant, John relaxes after dinner with Elliot Mintz, who was visiting
from America.     *Japan, summer 1977.*

Yoko waits outside the restaurant while John and Elliot put on their shoes.
*Japan, summer 1977.*

John, Yoko, and Elliot in Karuizawa.
*Japan, summer 1977.*

John, Elliot, and Yoko visit a temple. *Japan, summer 1977.*

John piles rocks as a form of prayer while visiting a temple. *Japan, summer 1977.*

Yoko and John in front of the Mampei Hotel.
*Japan, summer 1977.*

John Lennon.    *Japan, summer 1977.*

Yoko Ono.    *Japan, summer 1977.*

John and Sean in the garden of the Ono
family summer home, a short walk from
the Mampei Hotel. John is wearing a
*yukata* he bought in Tokyo.

*Japan, summer 1977.*

John and Yoko's mother, Isoko, in the
garden.

*Japan, summer 1977.*

Sean plays alone at a lookout point in Karuizawa.
While in Japan, he attended nursery school and
learned to speak some Japanese.

*Japan,*
*summer 1977.*

*Next page:* John and Yoko pose in front of the beautiful mountains of Karuizawa and take pictures of each other with John's Polaroid camera. John liked one of the photos so much he commissioned Andy Warhol to make it into a large silk screen as a gift for Yoko.

*Japan,*
*summer 1977.*

John and Yoko relax in a hotel room at the Mampei Hotel in Karuizawa. They liked the half-Japanese, half-Western atmosphere of this hotel.

*Japan,*
*summer 1977.*

Yoko, Sean, and John at the Mampei Hotel.    *Japan, summer 1977.*

Yoko, Sean, and John take a boat ride on a lake near Karuizawa.
*Japan, summer 1977.*

John lifts an unhappy Sean off a ride.     *Japan, summer 1977.*

John, Yoko, and Sean pose near the Shiraito Waterfall, a place they visited often.
*Japan, summer 1977.*

Yoko's young relatives and her mother, Isoko, spend the day with the Lennon
family. John organized the day's events whenever Yoko's relatives visited.
*Japan, summer 1977.*

John shows Sean how to throw a Frisbee on a sunny day.
Yoko listening attentively to Sean.     *Japan, summer 1977.*

John playing the guitar at a picnic.
*Japan, summer 1977.*

John plays with Sean during the picnic.

*Japan,*
*summer 1977.*

John holds Sean by the pool at the Hotel
Okura in Japan.

*Japan,*
*summer 1977.*

John plays with Sean in the pool.

*Japan, summer 1977.*

Sean takes a tumble into
the pool. Yoko at
poolside.

*Japan, summer 1977.*

John plays guitar to a laughing Sean in
the Hotel Okura, Tokyo.

*Japan,*
*summer 1977.*

*Winter 1977*

John, Yoko, and Julian Lennon sled
down a hill in Central Park. Julian
came from England to stay with
the Lennons during Christmas
vacation.

*New York City,
December 1977.*

John, Yoko, and Julian, bundled up against the cold.

*New York City, December 1977.*

John and Julian in
Central Park.

*New York City,
December 1977.*

John and Julian thaw out
in the kitchen of the
Dakota apartment.

*New York City,
December 1977.*

# Summer 1978

During early summer of 1978, John and Yoko chartered a small jet in Florida to fly to the Caribbean.

*Miami, Florida,*
*summer 1978.*

Sean, John and Yoko en route to Grand Cayman Island.

*Summer, 1978.*

The Lennon family returned to
Japan during the summer of 1978.
Here, John swims in pool of the
Hotel Okura in Tokyo.

*Japan,*
*August 1978.*

John plays with Sean in the hotel pool.
Sean is almost three years old here.

*Japan,*
*August 1978.*

John stops to fix Sean's goggles.

*Japan,*
*August 1978.*

John and a sleepy-looking Sean relax by
the pool.

*Japan,*
*August 1978.*

# Fall 1978

John and Sean, who shared the same birthday, blow out birthday candles together. John is thirty-eight and Sean is three.

*New York City,*
*October 9, 1978.*

Friends and neighbors at John and Sean's birthday party in Central Park's Tavern on the Green. *New York City, October 9, 1978.*

Sean watches John open a present.     *New York City, October 9, 1978.*

The birthday party included a magic show.    *New York City, October 9, 1978.*

# Winter 1978

John and Sean in the kitchen of the Dakota apartment.

*New York City, winter 1978.*

# Summer 1979

John, Sean, and Yoko pose for a family portrait in Japan. This was John's last visit to Karuizawa. During the summer of 1980, he and Yoko recorded their last album, *Double Fantasy,* and did not go to Japan.

*Japan, summer 1979.*

In a restaurant on the way to the lookout point in Karuizawa John shows Palaroid pictures to a hungry and uninterested Sean.

*Japan,*
*summer 1979.*

Sean eats buckwheat noodles with chopsticks.     *Japan, summer 1979.*

*Karuizawa, Japan*
*summer* 1979.

John, Yoko, and Sean go for a morning
walk in Karuizawa in the fog.

*Japan,*
*summer 1979.*

John Lennon, born
October 9, 1940, at
Oxford Street Maternity
Hospital, Liverpool,
England.

*Japan,
summer 1979.*

Yoko Ono, born
February 18, 1933, in
Tokyo, Japan.

*Japan,*
*summer 1979.*

Sean Taro Ono Lennon, born
October 9, 1975, at New York Hospital.

*Japan,*
*summer 1979.*

*Japan, summer 1979.*

John starting the long journey home on the train from Karuizawa to Tokyo.

*Japan,*
*summer 1979.*

# Afterword

It's been ten years since John Lennon died. It's hard to believe someone who touched so many people and who taught the importance of peace and love is gone. I wish these photographs were being published to commemorate his fiftieth birthday, instead of the tenth anniversary of his death.

The photographs in this collection were never intended for publication. Shot during the period John and Yoko referred to as "Silence of Love," these photos were meant for the Lennon family album, to be enjoyed by family and close friends. I'd like to express my gratitude to the members of the Ono-Lennon family for letting me share this special part of their family life with the public.

I first met the Lennon family in the middle of August 1976 during my third stay in New York. At the time, they were eating a macrobiotic diet, and they were also looking for an assistant. A friend of mine who also followed a natural foods diet told me about the opening and encouraged me to apply. I did, and ended up working for the Lennons for the next three years.

I started taking pictures of Sean when he was less than a year old, and, before long, John and Yoko began quite naturally to move into the frame. When the Lennons were in New York, I would arrive at the Dakota apartment at ten o'clock in the morning. Most

of the time John and Yoko would be in the kitchen relaxing, reading, or handling business affairs. John would read the *New York Times* or a book of philosophy. Sean would be playing somewhere within John's sight. Sometimes Sean and John would play Tarzan, hanging onto a rope attached to the ceiling of the playroom, which also had a big wooden jungle gym and a slide. When it was time for Sean's nap, from one to three in the afternoon, John and Yoko would go to their room. Their lifestyle was geared to Sean's schedule.

The Lennon family traveled often. They wanted Sean to see many different places, starting at a young age. My first trip with them took place only three days after I began working for them, when they visited their macrobiotics instructor in Boston. I drove the '71 Chrysler station wagon from New York, but even with a map I couldn't find the Copley Plaza Hotel where they were staying. John, who was sitting in the passenger seat, rolled down the window to ask people for directions. Each time he would say "Right, I'll ask in a French accent," or, "This time let's try a German accent." Yoko giggled in the back seat. He was so natural and open that the people on the sidewalk didn't realize who he was.

On the way back from Boston, I got lost on the unfamiliar highways. We could see the skyscrapers of

Manhattan towering before us, but no matter which road I took, I couldn't seem to get to Manhattan. John and Yoko were completely worn out from the trip and I felt panicky. For an hour and a half I tried different routes. When I finally found my way onto a familiar road, John, who had fallen asleep with his hat pulled over his face, woke up, smiled, and said, "So, we can finally get home? Thank goodness, eh Nishi?" I was relieved and touched by his patience and sense of humor. Within a week I realized that John Lennon was a good person, in the truest sense, and one I could admire for the rest of my life. Before I started working for the Lennons I knew only vaguely of John, as I had never been a Beatles fan, but I quickly learned that being with John made everyone feel good.

Once, when we were visiting Hong Kong we ate at a famous European restaurant. The service was so horrible I was ready to make a scene. John said, "Don't worry about it. You all leave ahead of me and then I'll turn the chairs and table over and run." We left him and waited outside, but he didn't come out. We were beginning to worry, when John came running out of the restaurant. When we asked him what happened, he triumphantly said, "Yeah, I did it. And I dropped a tea cup, making it look like an accident." Everyone roared with laughter.

In the summer of 1977 when we were staying in Karuizawa, Japan, a cat gave birth in the attic, and some of the kittens fell into the space between the walls. John heard the meowing inside the wall and called the manager. When the manager said that the wall couldn't be opened until the next day, John said, "If we don't get them out right away, they might die!"

He got permission to tear the wall open himself. Dripping with sweat, the two of us tore a hole in the wall and freed the kittens. For a while, these kittens were members of the Lennon family, although they had to be given away when we returned to America.

Although John was a truly open, kind, and witty person, there were times when I saw him sitting alone, when it seemed to me that he projected a powerful and unique presence. I couldn't help feeling at times that he was bigger than life, in a way that is hard for me to put into words.

In 1979, after an exhibition of my photographs of New York street scenes, I decided to return to Japan to have my photo exhibition in Tokyo. On my last day, John and Yoko gave me an engraved gold watch. This affectionate gift made me happy. In April, July, and November of 1980, John and Yoko called me and asked if I could come back. I had been trying to decide whether to stay in Japan, and when they called in November, I decided to return to New York in January. On December 8, 1980, John was killed. Amid the tragedy, I felt remorse that I hadn't returned sooner, and a deep regret that I never saw him again.

John, Yoko, and Sean's daily life had a gentleness that was based on love. For them, being a family meant working hard, every day, to appreciate and value one another. John and Yoko's family taught me that love is the foundation of peace. The kind of love that begins with the family can help us learn to value others. If people can feel the warmth of family love in this collection of photographs, I'll be happy.

Nishi Fumiya Saimaru